The RAFT and the YABBY

the land remembers water
people remember purpose

reeds take root quietly
but in time they change the whole water

HEATHER ANNE GORDON

This print edition
published in 2026 by Centred in Choice

Title: The Raft and the Yabby

Author © Heather Anne Gordon

First published by Centred in Choice
ABN 17 601 690 975

This book is a work of narrative nonfiction. It draws on real experiences of community volunteering and environmental restoration. Some details have been adapted to present the story in a narrative form and to respect personal privacy. Any resemblance to specific persons or events is used with permission from the individuals and respect for the communities that inspired the work.

A catalogue record for this book is available from the National Library of Australia
ISBN 978-1-7644711-8-3

Title: The Raft and the Yabby

Acknowledgements:
We acknowledge and respect the deep spiritual connection and the relationship that First Nations people have to Country.
Country takes in everything within the landscape – landforms, waters, air, trees, rocks, plants, animals, foods, medicines, minerals, stories, and special places.
Connections to Country include cultural practices, knowledge, songs, stories, dances, and art, as well as all people: past, present, and future.

Front Cover: Nicola Kngwarraye Butler
Yabby. 210mm x 297mm acrylic on canvas
https://nicolabutler.com/
Back Cover and First Reader: Sam Koerner
https://www.convertthedirt.au/
Internal Design: Karen Marree Engel

Published by Centred in Choice
Sharing Australian voices, stories, strategies and skills with the world.
https://centredinchoice.com
PO Box 448 Alice Springs NT 0871
Australia

About the Book

The Raft and the Yabby begins with a simple project beside a farm dam on Peramangk Country in the Tanunda Hills of South Australia

A small group gathers to build a floating raft of reeds to help restore the health of the water. What unfolds is more than an environmental story.

Through the quiet work of restoring a landscape, the book explores retirement, volunteering and the ways purpose can be rediscovered through community participation.

Conversations emerge naturally while people work side by side, reflecting the informal networks of care that exist in many communities.

Grounded in real places and experiences, *The Raft and the Yabby* offers a gentle reflection on land stewardship, wellbeing and the small acts of connection that help both people and landscapes recover over time.

Contents

Mateship, mud and making a wetland

Mick had been thinking about retirement long before he officially finished up.

Not with worry, but with quiet curiosity.

Not in the way some blokes talk about it; counting down days, circling the calendar, terrified of what comes next, but in a steadier way. He and Jane had planned it properly. They had always planned things properly.

They were not anxious planners, the sort who filled spreadsheets with projections and worst-case scenarios. It was more a habit built over years of partnership. They talked things through. They considered what mattered. Then they made a decision and got on with it.

Jane, with her calm patience and creative brilliance in the classroom, had spent decades teaching children with disabilities; seeing potential where others saw limits. She had a quiet way of shifting a room. Children who had been labelled difficult or unteachable often settled in her presence. She paid attention to small signals. She understood that learning did not always move in straight lines. Mick admired that about her.

His own working life had been different. Practical. Structured. Systems and routines. He had been known as steady, reliable, the sort of person who arrived early and left when the job was finished properly rather than when the clock suggested it might be time.

For many years he had also been a volunteer with the CFS. That commitment had shaped his summers more than anything else. Extreme fire danger days carried their own atmosphere; the hot wind before a front, the uneasy stillness in the bush, the radio chatter that never quite left your mind even when you were sitting at the kitchen table.

Mick understood heat, wind and risk in his bones.

Fire teaches a person something about patience and timing. You learn when to move fast and when to wait. You learn that landscapes hold memory. You learn that people do too.

So when the official last day of work came, there was no drama.

No farewell speech that lingered too long.

No emotional collapse on the drive home.

Just a quiet nod to the next season.

Retirement can unsettle some men. The structure falls away. The role changes. The quiet can grow too loud if there is nothing to step into.

Mick had watched it happen to others.

Blokes who had been defined by their title on a business card. Men who wandered the house, short-tempered or restless. Men who filled the silence with television because they did not know what else to do with it.

Some of them had been good workers too. Solid people. The sort who carried a workplace through busy periods without complaint.

But when the scaffolding of work disappeared, something in them shifted.

The days stretched.

Purpose became harder to locate.

Mick had wondered, briefly, if that would be him.

The first Monday morning after finishing work, he had woken at 5.30 anyway.

The house was still.

Jane asleep beside him.

No alarm.

No urgency.

Just a strange openness in the day.

He had lain there, listening to his own breathing.

Not anxious.

Just aware.

He had noticed the small sounds of the house in a way he usually didn't; the soft creak of timber adjusting to the morning temperature, a bird calling somewhere outside, the distant hum of a car passing along the road.

The day felt wide.

Unclaimed.

He had felt the faintest flicker of uncertainty.

Not fear exactly.

Just the question of where to place himself next.

He had eventually slipped out of bed and made coffee quietly in the kitchen, careful not to wake Jane. The early light had come through the window at an angle that made the garden look softer than usual.

It struck him then that mornings like this had always existed.

He had simply been elsewhere.

Jane had asked him later that week, gently, 'How are you travelling with it?'

She had not asked the question casually. Jane rarely asked anything casually. She was curious in a way that gave people time to answer properly.

Mick had considered the question.

Not quickly.

He had taken a moment, leaning against the kitchen bench, turning the thought over before speaking.

'I think,' he'd said slowly, 'I'm alright.'

He became aware, a moment later, that he hadn't asked her the same question.

Mick realised retirement was not the absence of work.

It was the freedom to choose it.

He could still fix things. Build things. Volunteer. Show up when someone needed an extra pair of hands. The difference now was that none of it came with a timesheet or a performance review.

Mick and Jane had Europe and Canada booked with old friends. Couples whose children had grown up together, whose lives had braided over decades of school fetes, footy finals and shared holidays.

The planning for that trip had been part of the long view they had taken toward retirement.

There would be travel.

There would be time.

But before departure lounges and passports, there was still life here.

Work worth doing.

The Barossa had a way of keeping people connected to place. Vineyards. Hills. Small towns where you recognised the same faces across years of Saturday morning errands.

And there were always projects underway somewhere.

On a cooler day between extreme fire danger warnings, Mick drove up into the Tanunda Hills to see his mate Sam.

He'd checked the fire danger, of course.

That habit was never going to leave him.

The sun was glaring through the windscreen, almost blinding him as the road wound upward through the dry hills. The eucalyptus along the roadside shimmered slightly in the heat.

The land looked tired but familiar.

Summer had settled in.

Mick drove with one hand resting loosely on the steering wheel, the other on the open window ledge.

The air coming through the window carried the dry scent of dust and gum leaves.

He knew roughly what Sam had in mind for the day.

Something to do with the dam.

Sam always had ideas.

Some of them involved a fair bit of work.

Mick didn't mind that.

Driving there not because he had to.

But because he wanted to.

And that, he realised as the road curved into the hills, might be the most important difference of all.

Clay-Coloured Water

Sam and Kate had bought their property knowing it was tired. The buildings needed work. The land needed more.

They recognised it as Peramangk Country.

The place had good bones though. That was the phrase Sam had used when they first walked the boundary together. Good bones.

The house stood solid enough. The paddocks still held shape beneath the weeds. The dam wall was intact, though bare. A place like this, Sam believed, did not need rescuing so much as patience.

Kate had agreed.

Land remembers what it once held.

Years of neglect had left the dam clay-coloured and stark, ringed by eucalyptus and *Acacia pycnantha* on the top of the dam wall but otherwise barren of plant life. The slopes were steep and raw where water had cut away the edges during heavy rain. Bird tracks stitched the soft margins where the clay dried and cracked.

Rabbit scats dotted the ground.

There were heavy hoof impressions too. Most likely feral deer, maybe feral goats, maybe someone's cattle wandering through when a boundary fence had failed somewhere uphill.

Kangaroo prints showed where they had come down cautiously for a drink, the marks of their tails dragging lightly behind them.

Even in its depleted state the dam was still a gathering point.

Animals always found water.

The surface itself looked opaque and thick, the colour of diluted brick dust. After rain it clouded further as the steep banks shed more clay into the basin.

It was water, yes.

But it was not yet a wetland.

It held potential.

It just needed intention.

Beneath the clay bank, something shifted.

The movement was small enough to go unnoticed from above.

A subtle displacement in the soft mud where the water met the slope. A faint tremor travelled through the sediment before settling again.

Stillness returned.

Sam had already installed sprinklers around the house in case of fire. CFS thinking instils skills. When you have seen what wind and embers can do, you plan for it. Pipes were buried where they needed to be. Pumps had been tested. Hoses lay coiled and ready in the shed.

But Sam and Kate's latest ambition was gentler.

A floating biofilter raft planted with aquatic reeds and sedges to begin cleaning and softening the dam. The idea had come from a mix of sources: permaculture discussions, wetland restoration examples, and Sam's habit of reading widely whenever something caught his interest.

The raft would sit just offshore, its plants anchored in coconut coir. Over time the roots would grow downward into the water, forming a dense curtain beneath the surface.

Sediment would cling to those roots.

Nutrients would be absorbed.

Microorganisms would colonise the tangle.

Water, slowly, would clear.

It would not happen quickly.

Regeneration rarely did.

But it was a step toward making the dam a permanent waterhole rather than just a seasonal basin.

Sam, Kate and Heather had already experimented with water on a smaller scale.

Near the back door of the house, an artificial fishpond had once sat stagnant and decorative, a relic of some earlier landscaping enthusiasm. With careful planting and adjustments to circulation, they had transformed it into a living, life-giving pond. Dragonflies had arrived first. Then water skaters. Small frogs followed once the water stabilised.

That success had shifted their thinking.

Next to the pond, the chlorine-filtered swimming pool now sat in quiet anticipation of its own transformation. One day it too would become a natural swimming pool, filtered by plants rather than chemicals.

It was, in Sam's words, a whole-property reimagining based on water.

Sam and Kate worked multiple jobs to earn their income. Mid-thirties, they were busy people with paid work and volunteer roles, juggling time in ways that would have exhausted them if they had stopped to calculate it too closely.

But projects like this one were not chores.

They were investments in the long future of the place.

Heather had retired from paid work more than ten years ago, yet she never described herself as retired.

The word suggested an ending.

A folding away.

She had simply stepped out of one structure and into another.

She lived a fairly reclusive life as a writer and artist, choosing her projects carefully, guarding her energy, contributing where it mattered.

At an event with Sam once, a government employee had looked her up and down, lingering on the silver of her hair before glancing at Sam's obvious energy and vigour.

The age difference between them.

His eyes dropped to the name tags pinned to their lapels, as though the small printed rectangles might clarify the relationship that his assumptions could not.

He searched for resemblance, for some genetic explanation for their ease with each other, and, finding none, asked abruptly what she did.

There it was.

The sorting mechanism at work.

The assumption. Age equalled absence. Grey hair meant retreat.

If she stood beside a younger man, surely there had to be a family explanation.

'I'm an artist, author and children's book creator,' Heather replied, steady as you like.

She surprised herself with the firmness of it.

Sam grinned beside her.

The government bloke blinked, momentarily dislodged from his tidy categories.

They had laughed about it later in the car.

Not cruelly.

Just knowingly.

There was no blood tie between them, no shared last name, no inherited features.

What bound them was older and more deliberate than genetics.

Years of conversation.

Shared projects.

Disagreements that sharpened thinking.

Trust earned slowly.

Sam valued her experience.

Heather valued his momentum.

Neither of them needed to explain that to anyone.

Retirement, as far as Heather was concerned, was a bureaucratic term.

Contribution was the only measure that counted.

Heather volunteered too. Not regularly nowadays. Sporadically as her health allowed. She knew volunteering was not charity.

It was reciprocity.

Sam had called Heather for plant advice.

She had researched and sourced *Juncus pallidus*, *Carex tereticaulis* and *Phragmites australis* from the Barossa Bushgardens.

Good, tough plants.

Indigenous.

Hardy.

Plants that belonged.

Plants that could anchor the dam edges and begin rebuilding a living margin between land and water.

Kate, practical and organised, was running logistics for the day, as she did for most things.

She knew where everything was stored.

There were gluten-free biscuits and chai waiting in the kitchen.

There was 'Little Red', their EV, ready to ferry tools and materials from shed to dam.

There were twenty-litre drums standing by for buoyancy if the raft needed them.

Buckets. Spades. Secateurs. Twine.

All the quiet infrastructure of a working day.

There was a plan.

And beneath the clay-coloured water, unnoticed by the people standing on the bank above, something shifted again in the mud.

Not disturbed. Just aware.

The Raft Takes Shape

The raft components were classic Sam. He'd assembled repurposed materials found around the property. PVC pipe for the frame. Shade cloth stretched taut across the base. Coconut coir purchased from a hydroponic tomato grower to cradle the plants.
Nothing flashy.

Just resourceful.

Sam had a particular eye for things that still had usefulness left in them. Where someone else might see leftover pipe or discarded fittings, Sam saw the beginnings of a structure. A frame waiting to be assembled. The practical satisfaction of solving a problem with what was already at hand.

Mick loved the potential of it immediately.

There is something deeply satisfying about building something that floats. Something that will work quietly long after you step away.

The raft would not ask for applause. It would simply sit on the water doing its work, season after season, roots stretching down into the dam while birds perched above it.

They measured and cut. Tied and tightened. Adjusted and rebalanced.

Sam checked corners with the careful eye of someone who had built plenty of things outdoors and knew that wind and water had a way of testing weaknesses. Mick tightened knots where needed. Kate held the frame steady while the shade cloth was stretched and secured.

Heather watched the process with interest, occasionally offering a practical observation from her seat on an overturned crate.

The rhythm of the work settled quickly.

Measure.

Cut.

Hold.

Tie.

Stand back and check.

Then adjust.

When it was ready, they carried the raft from the shade of the shed over to the dam, along the banks and down the steep sides to the water.

The slope demanded care. Clay underfoot could be treacherous once it loosened.

The raft slid onto the clay-coloured water with a gentle slurp.

It rocked once.

Then steadied.

Below the surface the water darkened where the shade of the raft fell.

The disturbance travelled downward through the water column.

Mud trembled slightly where it lay undisturbed on the dam floor.

Then everything stilled again.

Kate and Heather had already removed the coconut coir from the plastic bags, sorting the strings used for the tomato growing and the plastic into a bucket ready for the landfill bin. They worked methodically, separating the natural fibre from the synthetic leftovers.

The coconut coir was now in big tubs and buckets ready to be added to the raft.

It had the faint earthy smell of dried husk and greenhouse humidity.

Mick waded in barefoot. His retirement boots, old rubber thongs, discarded on the bank.

The mud was cool between his toes.

He hadn't expected how much he would enjoy that.

For years he had worked in boots. Steel caps. Thick soles separating him from whatever surface he stood on. The sensation of bare feet pressing into soft clay felt unexpectedly grounding.

The mud yielded slightly. Then held.

The sensation slowed something inside him.

There was something about cold mud and warm sun that made thinking unnecessary.

He shifted his weight to step forward.

The mud moved again beneath his heel.

Not quite the sensation of sinking.

Something else.

A faint disturbance.

Mick paused for a moment.

Probably trapped air, he thought.

Or something alive.

He shrugged and continued.

Below him, the pressure of his step travelled outward through the clay.

Something beneath the mud remained still.

Waiting.

Mick added the coconut coir to the raft.

A thin layer, as directed by Sam.

More was needed.

Kate prepared to go back to the shed for another load. Mick offered to accompany her.

He exited the water carefully, the mud slippery and dangerous. Clay had a way of releasing its grip at exactly the wrong moment.

Heather asked about Mick's phone as he slipped, then wobbled, in the mud.

Mick steadied himself.

'Back at the shed,' he said.

That was a relief.

Heather moved back from the edge, hoping not to be splashed by Mick.

Or worse still, grabbed for balance. Although she couldn't imagine Mick doing that.

He was too careful.

For a split second, as Mick wobbled, the old instinct to prove himself flared.

That instinct socialised in men not to show weakness. Not to show age. Not to let a misstep turn into a moment of concern.

Then it passed.

Heather joked about her rescue skills from being a swimming and water safety instructor being no longer up to standard.

Mick laughed.

The moment dissolved.

Mick and Kate drove off in Little Red.

The small electric vehicle hummed quietly up the track toward the shed, its tyres crunching over dry gravel.

Heather waited at the water's edge, breathing in the fragrance of the eucalypts as the day warmed.

The air carried the warm resin scent of gum leaves and dry grass.

Her eyes closed briefly to better hear the birdlife in the distance.

Magpies.

A wattlebird somewhere higher up the slope.

The faint chatter of small finches moving through the shrubs.

Sam came around from the other side of the dam where he'd anchored the raft with rope and some rocks.

They walked together toward the small island on the southern edge.

Sam pointed out where he imagined reeds might one day thicken along the margins.

Heather listened to Sam's plans.

Then Heather said, 'Mick wondered if there might be yabbies. But it looks barren. I can't imagine anything living in this silty water. Have you seen any small holes for yabbies along the edge?'

'I'd be surprised,' said Sam. 'Although there must have been at one time. There are a couple of metal traps that I threw up on the bank.'

Heather squinted across the dam at the rusting rectangular shapes flung against the steeply sloping dam wall.

'Yeah, they look illegal,' said Heather. 'I think they were banned because rakali and turtles can enter the trap and drown.'

'I'd love it if there were turtles,' said Sam.

'I'd love for there to be swamp rats,' said Heather. 'They are the cutest.'

'There would have to be a lot more vegetation before swamp rats would choose to live here,' said Sam. 'I will be happy if there are more birds.'

'I'll have to put in a request to management for a bird hide,' said Heather with a sideways glance at Sam.

'We will discuss that with Kate,' said Sam.

All of them understood that land regeneration mirrors human renewal.

You prepare conditions.

You introduce the right elements.

Then you wait.

Kate and Mick returned.

More coconut coir was added by Mick to the raft, standing in the water to his knees, revelling in the cool as the sun warmed his shoulders.

Freeboard was checked.

The drums waited nearby in case more lift was needed, but in the end Heather claimed one as her supervisory throne. She sat on it near the waterline.

From there she had a clear view of the raft and the bank.

Heather and Kate had already removed the plants from their plastic tubes.

They always worked companionably on projects.

Most often with no need for chat.

They'd worked together on a collaborative art project a few years back, quietly gluing fabric to create the ruffles of fur on a megafauna creature. The hours had passed with the comfortable rhythm of shared concentration.

Anticipating each other's needs.

Fitting tea breaks around glue refills.

Whereas when Sam and Heather worked together there was constant banter as Sam bounced ideas off Heather, valuing her experience and their long-term relationship.

They were loud, sweary, uninhibited in their discussions.

Heather and Jane had worked together on art projects too.

Mick had been in the background, steadily supportive of Jane's creativity.

Heather could appreciate that.

She checked whether Mick was willing to participate in an art workshop about bees during July.

He asked a few questions.

Heather was mostly reassuring.

Perhaps a bit vague.

Heather asked, 'You going all right with retirement?'

'Yeah. Better than I expected,' Mick responded.

For Mick there was a strange liberation in retirement.

The boots come off.

The pace changes.

No one is watching the clock.

He realised how long it had been since he'd worked without performance reviews, without targets, without anyone measuring the outcome.

Here, the only measure was whether the raft floated properly and the plants settled into their new home.

Mick planted *Juncus* and *Carex* through the coir, making small slits in the shade cloth beneath with a sharp knife.

He pressed *Phragmites* in firmly.

Listened to Heather's quiet instructions.

Sam, meanwhile, used a drill attachment to create planting holes along the dam's edge and set more *Phragmites* into the clay bank.

Kate watered them in with the dam's own silty water.

She moved methodically along the bank, not rushing.

Each plant received its share.

'They'll need watering again this summer,' she said.

It wasn't doubt.

It was commitment.

Kate caught up with Sam's planting of the reeds.

She bent to get more water from the dam in the bucket.

Their eyes met.

'Reckon we're mad?' Sam asked.

'Always,' Kate replied. 'But we're consistent.'

At one point Heather and Kate stood side by side, hands on hips.

'For balance,' they insisted, laughing, as they steadied themselves on the steep slope.

Not bossy at all.

Although Sam referred to them both as his bosses.

Mick climbed the steep edge of the dam to the embankment where dead *Acacia* branches lay on the ground. He carried some down to the raft, placing them carefully across the frame to provide resting perches for birds.

Above the waterline the raft now looked less like a construction project and more like a small floating island.

Sam entertained the group with a story about what might happen if a pelican decided to nest on the raft.

Heather rolled her eyes.

Kate laughed.

Mick looked out across the water.

The dam still looked barren.

But now it had intention.

And beneath the quiet surface, in the cool clay where the disturbance of the morning had finally settled, something shifted again in the mud.

Roots Beneath the Water

On the surface, it was a raft.

A rectangle of pipe and shade cloth floating just offshore, its edges softened by the first clusters of reeds pushed into coconut coir.

From a distance it looked almost modest.

A small experiment.

Something temporary.

Underneath, it was something else.

The raft was not only a floating island of plants that would grow a curtain of roots to act as a biofilter for the water. It was also the beginning of a change in the dam itself.

Over time those roots would stretch downward through the water column. They would catch sediment. They would host colonies of microorganisms invisible to the naked eye. Insects would lay eggs among the stems. Small creatures would find shelter in the tangled fibres.

What looked simple on the surface would become complex underneath.

Regeneration rarely announced itself loudly.

It built quietly, layer by layer.

Retirement can unsettle men.

The structure falls away. The role changes. The quiet can grow too loud if there is nothing to step into.

Some men shrink.

Some drift.

Some miss the daily usefulness more than they admit.

Mick did not miss it.

Because he had not stepped away from purpose.

He had stepped toward it.

The difference was subtle but important.

CFS still called when needed. Fire seasons did not disappear just because someone reached retirement age. Experience mattered. The younger volunteers appreciated someone who had stood in hot wind before and knew how quickly conditions could turn.

The Bushgardens would soon have two new volunteers.

Jane with her deep knowledge of learning and inclusion.

Mick with his steady hands and willingness to lift, dig and fix.

Places like the Barossa Bushgardens ran on that sort of quiet commitment. Volunteers who showed up. People who understood that land stewardship was a long conversation rather than a short project.

Mick told Heather about being involved in planting the CFS Firewise Garden at the Bushgardens.

'That was a fair while back now,' he said, pressing another plant firmly into the coir.

Heather nodded.

'Still there,' she said. 'Still doing its job.'

The Firewise Garden had been designed to demonstrate how thoughtful planting could reduce fire risk around homes. Low fuel loads. Strategic spacing. Plants chosen for their moisture retention and resilience.

Practical knowledge shared with the wider community.

Mick had always liked that about the Bushgardens.

Knowledge turned outward.

Heather talked about some of the things she had achieved in retirement, despite physical limitations.

Writing.

Art.

Collaborations that moved slowly but mattered deeply.

Retirement, for her, had not been withdrawal. It had been recalibration. Learning how to direct energy carefully rather than spreading it too thinly.

The conversation drifted easily between them as Mick worked.

There would be time for travel for Mick and Jane.

Time for friendship.

Time for projects that mattered.

Standing knee-deep in a muddy dam on a cool Tanunda morning, Mick felt none of the unease that others had warned him about.

He felt useful.

Calm.

Connected.

The dam water lapped quietly around his knees as he worked.

Mick understood something else too.

The body remembers usefulness.

It steadies the mind.

Lifting the raft.

Tying knots.

Pressing plants into coir.

These were not chores.

They were anchors.

He drove Little Red up and down the track like a kid with a new toy, ferrying tools and plants between the shed and the dam.

The small electric motor hummed softly as it climbed the slope.

Mick laughed easily.

There was no rush.

That was another change retirement allowed.

Work could unfold at the pace it needed rather than the pace demanded by a timetable.

Sam spoke about installing a camera to record visitors to the dam.

'Just a motion sensor,' he explained. 'See who comes at night.'

Kangaroos.

Foxes.

Maybe echidnas wandering through the undergrowth.

Perhaps even owls swooping low across the water once the reeds established and insects began to gather there.

The dam might become a small hub of activity again.

'We'll make it worth their while,' Sam said.

And that was the point.

Regeneration is slow.

It does not announce itself.

It begins with small acts.

A planted reed.

Shared biscuits.

A mate showing up on a cool day.

Sam walked around to the far side of the dam to anchor the raft properly, looping the rope around a half-submerged rock he'd scouted earlier.

The rock sat just beneath the surface, visible only when the light struck it at the right angle.

Sam crouched, reached down and secured the rope with careful knots.

Heather didn't bother to follow.

She stood with her hands on her hips, squinting against the sunlight despite her sunglasses.

'Bit more slack,' she called.

Sam adjusted without looking up.

He knew the tone.

Not criticism.

Calibration.

'You want it to drift or behave?' he shot back.

'Drift with purpose,' she replied.

He grinned.

The phrase suited the day.

He tightened the knot once more, then stood back, assessing the line of the raft against the gentlest breeze crossing the water.

They didn't need to say much.

Years of working alongside each other had reduced instructions to fragments.

He trusted her eye.

She trusted his hands.

If she said the angle was off, he adjusted it.

If he said the bank wouldn't hold, she didn't argue.

Above the surface the raft looked steady now, its corners aligned with the faint movement of wind across the dam.

But below the surface something else was beginning.

The first pale threads of root had already begun to press downward through the coconut coir.

They reached slowly into the water beneath the raft, searching.

Below them the water cooled slightly in the shade.

The mud on the dam floor held its quiet memory of the morning's disturbance.

Something shifted again in the clay.

Not alarmed.

Curious perhaps, if such a word could be used.

A faint movement through the sediment.

The roots would take time to reach that depth.

But the change had begun.

Above the waterline Sam wiped his hands on his shorts and stepped back to admire the raft.

It rocked slightly once.

Then steadied into place.

Heather watched the angle of the rope.

'That'll do,' she said.

Sam nodded.

'Reckon so.'

And that was that.

No ceremony.

No praise.

Just the quiet recognition of something done properly.

A small change introduced into the world.

And the patience to see what might follow.

The First Sign

They finished with chai and gluten-free biscuits even though it was nearly lunchtime.

Kate had set the mugs out on the back of the EV earlier, knowing that projects like this always ended the same way, with everyone suddenly aware they were thirsty and a little hungry after hours of steady work.

The chai was sweet and warm, the biscuits crumbly enough to leave traces of almond meal on fingers and shirts.

They stood or perched wherever was comfortable. On the bank, on a drum, on the edge of the tailgate, looking out over the dam.

The raft sat quietly offshore, its green tufts already softening the water's edge.

What had begun the morning as pipe and shade cloth now resembled a small floating island. The young reeds leaned slightly in the breeze, their narrow leaves catching the sunlight.

The new plantings along the bank looked fragile.

But they were anchored.

Roots pressed into clay.

Water seeping slowly around them.

They would settle.

A monarch butterfly appeared before they left.

Just one.

Hovering.

Considering.

The orange wings flickered against the pale sky as it moved slowly across the dam, drifting first toward the reeds along the bank and then circling back toward the raft.

Heather noticed first.

'There you go,' she said softly.

Sam followed her gaze.

He didn't speak straight away.

Just watched the small flicker of orange testing the air above the raft, as if weighing the promise of it.

The butterfly hovered briefly above the new plants, then lifted slightly on a warm current of air.

Sam glanced at Heather.

She gave the smallest nod.

Not triumph.

Not surprise.

Just acknowledgement.

They both understood what it meant.

Not that the work was finished.

But that it had begun.

Insects were often the first to arrive when a landscape shifted. They moved lightly through the world, sampling new places without hesitation.

If the conditions were right, they stayed.

Sam bent to pick up the empty tubs and stack them in the back of Little Red. The plastic containers knocked together with a hollow clatter as he placed them down.

Heather stepped back from the edge of the dam.

No need to say anything more.

Kate saw the exchange and smiled, understanding more than was said.

She had learned long ago that Sam and Heather communicated as much through pauses as through words.

Kate moved toward the driver's side of Little Red, washing clay from her hands before climbing in.

Heather followed and settled into the passenger seat.

The small electric vehicle hummed faintly as it powered on.

Mick remained where he was.

He stood with his hands on his hips.

Not for balance.

Just because it felt right.

He looked across the clay-coloured water.

The dam was still cloudy. The banks still raw. The reeds newly planted and vulnerable.

But he could see it now.

Not what it was.

What it would be.

A permanent wetland.

Frogs calling from the margins at dusk.

Birds arriving in the morning.

Dragonflies patrolling the surface once the water cleared.

Clean water.

The swimming pool near the house one day chemical-free.

The house safer with water close by.

The land held more gently because two people had decided to commit to it together.

Sam and Kate had chosen this place knowing it would take work.

They had chosen the long path.

Mick admired that.

He thought about the way landscapes slowly reveal themselves when someone begins paying attention to them.

Water changes first.

Then insects.

Then birds.

Then the deeper rhythms of soil and root.

And himself.

Not retired and fading.

But retired and re-rooted.

Jane would love this, he thought.

She would understand the symbolism immediately.

The way you create the conditions and then step back.

The way you trust growth.

He imagined telling her about the morning when he got home.

The raft.

The reeds.

The butterfly.

And the unexpected pleasure of standing barefoot in cool mud.

He smiled slightly at the thought.

Jane would laugh and say that sounded suspiciously like a beauty treatment.

Maybe it was therapy.

Something in the simple physical work had settled him.

The body remembers what usefulness feels like.

That was the thing people rarely explained properly about retirement.

It wasn't about stopping.

It was about choosing where your effort mattered.

As they packed up, Sam walked over and clapped Mick lightly on the shoulder.

'Good day's work.'

Mick smiled.

'Yeah,' Mick said. 'It is.'

Sam looked out over the water too.

The raft moved gently in the faint breeze, the rope line holding it just where they had planned.

'Give it a year,' Sam said. 'You won't recognise the place.'

Mick believed him.

Retirement, he realised, was not a shrinking of the world.

It was an expansion of it.

If you kept saying yes.

Mick watched as Little Red began its slow climb up the track toward the house, Kate driving carefully over the uneven ground.

Sam followed a moment later, heading toward the shed to return the remaining tools.

Mick lingered a little longer.

The dam had grown quiet again.

The butterfly had drifted off toward the trees.

The breeze softened.

Below the surface, where the shade of the raft cooled the water slightly, the first thin threads of root had begun their slow descent through the coir.

They reached downward, patient and pale.

In the clay below, something moved.

The disturbance was slight.

A gentle shifting through the mud where the morning's footsteps had long since settled.

The creature tested the water cautiously, pushing forward through the soft sediment.

Above it, the water held the faint shadow of the new raft.

Roots would come.

Shade.

Insects.

Life returning in increments too small for people to notice day by day.

The creature moved again, then settled.

Waiting.

Above the waterline, the dam looked almost the same as it had that morning.

But the change had already begun.

Beneath the quiet water, something was already moving.

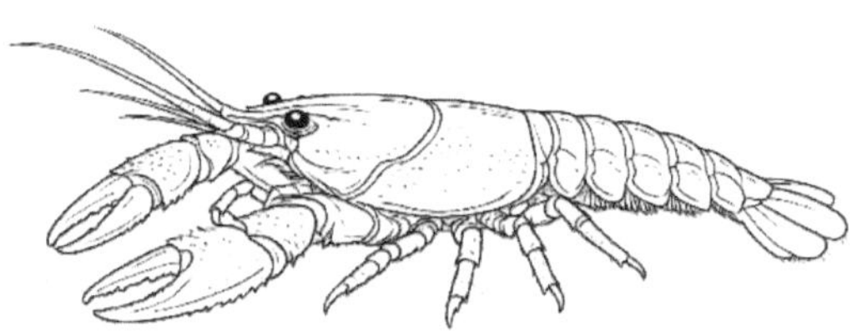

This book is designed as a flexible resource, with sections usable independently.

This resource works best when each participant has their own copy, allowing everyone to follow along and contribute to discussions.

Informal Support Networks, Side-by-Side Wellbeing and Men's Mental Health

Introduction

Conversations about men's mental health often focus on formal interventions such as counselling, crisis services and clinical care. These services are essential and can be life-saving.

Yet alongside these systems there exists another form of support that is less visible but equally important: informal networks that allow men to remain connected, purposeful and socially engaged.

A small land regeneration project in the Tanunda Hills of South Australia offers a useful metaphor for understanding how these informal systems operate. On the surface the project involved a practical task; building a floating raft of reeds to help restore the ecological health of a farm dam.

Beneath that simple activity, however, the project revealed something deeper about the ways men support one another through life transitions such as retirement.

Like the floating raft itself, informal support networks may appear simple from the outside. Underneath, they provide stabilising structures that quietly sustain wellbeing.

Retirement and the Loss of Structure

Retirement represents a significant transition in many men's lives. For decades work provides structure, routine and a sense of identity. Daily interactions with colleagues, shared tasks and the satisfaction of completing practical work form an important part of social and emotional life.
When that structure disappears, the change can be disorienting.

Some men adapt quickly, moving into new forms of activity and community involvement. Others experience a loss of purpose that can contribute to isolation, frustration or declining mental health.

Research consistently shows that men are less likely than women to seek formal psychological support, even when they are struggling.

This does not mean men do not need support. Rather, it suggests that the forms of support that feel accessible and meaningful may differ.

The dam restoration project illustrates one way that support can emerge organically through shared work.

Retirement also changes the daily experience of those closest to the person who has stopped working.

Partners, spouses and household members absorb significant shifts in routine, space and rhythm when someone retires.

Their own needs during this transition can go unexamined, particularly if attention remains focused on supporting the person who has left the workforce.

Conversations about retirement and wellbeing are strengthened when they make room for both people's experience of the change.

The Dam as a Metaphor for Transition

When Sam and Kate first purchased their property, the dam on the land appeared depleted.

Years of neglect had left the water cloudy and the banks bare.

The dam still held water, and animals still visited it, but it lacked the complex plant life that would normally stabilise a healthy wetland system.

It held potential.

It simply needed intention.

The condition of the dam reflects something that can happen in human lives during major transitions.

The underlying capacity for renewal remains present, but the structures that support it may need to be rebuilt.

In ecological restoration, small interventions can create conditions that allow a system to recover over time.

The floating reed raft introduced to the dam was one such intervention.

The Raft: A Structure That Supports

The raft constructed on the dam was modest in appearance. A simple frame of pipe and shade cloth supporting young reeds planted in coconut fibre. Over time the plants will send roots down into the water, creating a dense curtain that filters sediment and improves water quality.

What appears simple above the surface becomes complex below it.

This offers a powerful metaphor for informal support networks among men.

A working bee, a volunteer project, a shed workshop or a group of mates helping each other on small tasks may appear casual or purely practical.

Yet these environments create spaces where connection and conversation occur naturally.

The activity itself becomes the organising structure.

In the case of the dam, several people gathered to build and plant the raft.

The work required measuring, lifting, tying knots, transporting materials and planting reeds.

Each task contributed to the practical goal of improving the dam.

At the same time, the work created opportunities for conversation.

Not forced discussion, but the kind of quiet exchange that occurs when people are focused on a shared task.

Side-by-Side Wellbeing

Much discussion of mental health support assumes that meaningful conversations happen face-to-face, often in formal settings such as therapy sessions.

While this model is valuable and necessary, it does not always reflect how many men naturally communicate.

Men often talk more easily side-by-side rather than face-to-face.

Fishing, repairing equipment, building something together, driving somewhere or working on a project can provide the social environment where conversation emerges without pressure. The shared activity reduces the intensity of direct emotional disclosure while still allowing reflection and connection.

This pattern is sometimes referred to as **side-by-side wellbeing**.

The dam project illustrated this dynamic clearly.

Conversations about retirement, purpose and future plans unfolded while people were planting reeds, ferrying materials and adjusting the raft.

No one had gathered specifically to talk about mental health, yet the environment allowed participants to reflect openly on life transitions.

Standing knee-deep in cool mud while planting reeds, one participant observed that the body remembers usefulness.

Physical engagement — lifting, digging, tying knots — can quiet the mind and restore a sense of competence.

Such experiences can be deeply stabilising during times of change.

Informal Support as Prevention

Informal networks like this do not replace professional mental health care. Rather, they can serve as preventative support systems that strengthen resilience and reduce isolation.

Just as the reed raft improves the dam gradually rather than instantly, informal support structures contribute to wellbeing over time.

Several factors make these environments particularly valuable:

Purpose

Shared projects provide a sense of contribution. Participants are not simply talking about wellbeing; they are creating something tangible together.

Routine Interaction
Regular contact with others reduces isolation and reinforces social connection.

Non-judgemental Conversation
Discussion occurs naturally and without the pressure to disclose personal difficulties unless someone chooses to.

Intergenerational Exchange
Projects that involve people of different ages allow experience and energy to complement each other.

In the dam project, the collaboration between people at different life stages created a balanced dynamic. Younger participants contributed momentum and physical energy. Older participants offered experience, perspective and technical knowledge.

The Hidden Life Beneath the Surface

During the dam project there was also speculation about whether yabbies might already live in the water.

The dam appeared barren, yet beneath the clay-coloured surface life might still be present.

This image offers another metaphor for men's wellbeing.

From the outside, a person may appear calm or functional while internal struggles remain hidden. At the same time, beneath that surface there may also be resilience, adaptability and the capacity for renewal.

The presence of a supportive environment can allow that resilience to emerge.

In ecological terms, the raft does not create life in the dam. It simply creates conditions where life that may already exist can flourish.

Informal support networks operate in much the same way.

They provide conditions where people can reconnect with purpose and community.

When Formal Support Is Needed

While informal networks play an important role in supporting wellbeing, they are not a substitute for professional care when serious mental health challenges arise.

Counselling, psychological therapy and crisis support services provide structured environments where individuals can explore complex emotions, trauma and mental health conditions in depth.

The relationship between informal support and formal therapy should therefore be understood as complementary rather than competing.

Informal networks may:

- *help individuals maintain wellbeing during life transitions*
- *reduce stigma around discussing personal challenges*
- *encourage people to seek professional support when needed*
- *provide ongoing social support alongside formal treatment.*

In many cases, individuals who feel connected to community networks may find it easier to take the step of seeking professional help if difficulties escalate.

Regeneration as a Long Process

Ecological restoration teaches an important lesson about patience.

The reed raft placed in the dam will not transform the water overnight. Roots will take months to develop. Sediment will slowly accumulate around them. Insects and birds will arrive gradually as the habitat improves.

Over time, however, the cumulative effect of these small changes can reshape the entire system.

Social wellbeing operates in a similar way.

Regular interaction, shared work and mutual support create environments where individuals can remain connected and resilient through changing life circumstances.

The dam restoration project demonstrates how modest actions, such as building a raft, planting reeds, sharing tea after a morning's work, can contribute to broader wellbeing.

Conclusion

Men's mental health is often discussed primarily in terms of crisis intervention and formal therapy. These services remain critically important and must continue to be supported and expanded.

At the same time, the quieter structures of everyday life deserve greater recognition.

Community projects, volunteering, environmental restoration, men's sheds and informal working groups all create opportunities for side-by-side wellbeing. These environments allow men to maintain purpose, connection and identity during life transitions such as retirement.

Like the floating raft on the dam, such structures may appear simple. Beneath the surface, however, they support complex networks of connection that stabilise the social ecosystem.

Sometimes the most effective support begins with something as ordinary as showing up to help with a small job.

A planted reed.

Shared biscuits.

A conversation that emerges naturally while working beside someone else.

Over time, these small acts can help restore balance. Not only to landscapes, but to the lives of the people who care for them.

Book Club Questions
The Raft and the Yabby

1. The story begins with Mick reflecting on retirement and the loss of structure that work can provide.
   What did you notice about the way he approached this transition?

2. Jane is described as someone with "calm patience and creative brilliance" who spent decades teaching children with disabilities. She is clearly a perceptive and caring partner. Yet the story shows her mostly through Mick's eyes. What do you imagine retirement has meant for Jane? Her routines, her space, her own sense of transition? Whose experience is most visible in the story, and whose is quieter?

3. The dam initially appears barren and depleted.
   How does the landscape mirror the personal transitions taking place in the story?

4. The floating raft is a small intervention designed to begin restoring the dam.
   What might the raft symbolise in terms of community, friendship, or support?

5. The story suggests that a yabby may already be living beneath the mud, unseen.
   What do you think the yabby represents?

6. Much of the conversation in the story happens while the characters are working side-by-side.
   Why do you think practical work can sometimes make it easier for people to talk?

7. The book highlights the role of volunteering and community participation.
   Have you seen similar examples in your own community?

8. The line *'the body remembers usefulness'* appears during the work at the dam.
   What does this phrase mean to you?

9. The butterfly appears near the end of the story as the group finishes their work.
   Why do you think the author chose that moment as a sign of change.

10. The story suggests that purpose and wellbeing can grow through small actions rather than dramatic change.
    Do you agree with this idea?

11. Mick reflects that retirement is not the absence of work but the freedom to choose it. Jane is also moving into a new season of life.
    What meaningful work or connection might she be seeking, or already quietly doing, that the story doesn't show us?

12. The book explores both environmental regeneration and human wellbeing.
    How do you see these two ideas connected?

13. The characters come from different life stages and experiences.
    What role does intergenerational collaboration play in the story?

14. The book closes with the idea that change has already begun beneath the water.
    Where do you see similar beginnings of change in your own life or community?

15. What is the "raft" in your life?
    In the story, the raft is a small structure that quietly supports change over time.
    What people, places, or activities in your life play a similar role in helping you stay grounded or purposeful?

16. What might be the "yabby beneath the mud"?
    The story suggests that life and resilience may already exist beneath the surface, even when things appear quiet or uncertain. Where have you seen hidden strength or potential in yourself, others, or a community?

17. Where in your life or community might change already be beginning? Even if it isn't visible yet?
    The dam looks much the same at the end of the day, yet something has already begun beneath the water.
    What small actions or relationships might be quietly shaping the future?

Yes, it is important to read the book before the Book Club meeting.

Drift With Purpose

Men's Wellbeing, Volunteering and the Value of Side-by-Side Community Work

Introduction

Across Australia, community organisations such as Men's Sheds, Landcare groups and volunteer emergency services provide something more than practical outcomes.

While they repair equipment, restore landscapes or respond to emergencies, they also create environments where social connection, purpose and wellbeing develop naturally.

These spaces rarely describe themselves as mental health programs. Yet they play an important role in supporting wellbeing, particularly for men navigating life transitions such as retirement, redundancy or changing family circumstances.

A small land regeneration project in the Tanunda Hills of South Australia illustrates how this kind of support can emerge through shared work.

On the surface, the task was simple: constructing a floating reed raft to help restore the ecological health of a farm dam.

Beneath that activity, however, the project reflected many of the same dynamics that make Men's Sheds, Landcare groups and volunteer organisations valuable for community wellbeing.

The lesson is straightforward. Purposeful activity and social connection often work best together.

Life Transitions and the Need for Purpose

Major life transitions can disrupt the structures that previously organised daily life. Retirement is a particularly significant example. For many men, work has provided not only income but also identity, routine and regular social contact.

When work ends, those structures can disappear suddenly.

Some people adapt quickly, replacing formal work with volunteering, travel or new projects.

Others experience a loss of purpose that can lead to isolation or declining mental health.

Research consistently shows that men are less likely than women to seek formal psychological support, even when they may benefit from it.

This does not mean men do not need support.

Rather, it highlights the importance of environments where connection and conversation occur in ways that feel natural.

Community volunteering and shared projects often provide exactly that environment.

The Power of Side-by-Side Wellbeing

Much discussion about mental health assumes that meaningful conversations occur face-to-face, often in structured settings such as counselling sessions.

While professional support is essential and should always be available when needed, it is not the only way people build resilience.

Many men communicate more comfortably side-by-side rather than face-to-face.

Working together on a practical task, such as repairing a piece of machinery, planting trees, building something or restoring a landscape, allows conversation to unfold gradually and without pressure.

The shared activity provides the focus, reducing the intensity that sometimes accompanies direct emotional discussion.

This dynamic is often visible in Men's Sheds.

People may arrive to work on projects, sharpen tools or fix equipment.

Over time, the shed becomes a place where friendships form and conversations emerge naturally.

Landcare and environmental volunteering operate in a similar way.

Planting trees, restoring waterways or managing local reserves requires collaboration. Participants contribute their skills while also building relationships with others who share a commitment to caring for place.

In both settings, the work itself becomes the structure that holds the group together.

A Case Study: Restoring a Farm Dam

The dam restoration project in the Tanunda Hills demonstrates how these principles operate in practice.

The dam had become degraded after years of neglect. Its water was cloudy with suspended clay and the banks were largely bare of plant life. While the dam still held water, it lacked the ecological complexity needed to support a healthy wetland.

The restoration plan was modest but practical: build a floating raft planted with aquatic reeds and sedges.

Over time the roots of these plants would grow down into the water, forming a natural filtration system that would gradually improve water quality.

Constructing the raft required a range of small tasks. Materials were gathered from around the property. A frame was assembled using PVC pipe and shade cloth. Coconut fibre was prepared to hold the plants. Reeds were planted both on the raft and along the dam's edges.

The work was straightforward but collaborative.

People measured and cut materials. They carried the raft down the bank to the water.

They stood knee-deep in mud while positioning plants.

Tools and materials were ferried back and forth between the shed and the dam.

During this process, conversation unfolded easily.

Topics ranged from volunteering experiences to retirement and future plans. There was no formal agenda and no expectation that anyone should share personal reflections. Yet the environment created space for those reflections to emerge naturally.

One participant described the experience simply: *the body remembers usefulness.*

Physical work such as lifting, tying knots, planting reeds, created a sense of calm and purpose.

In that setting, conversation about life transitions became easier.

Informal Networks as Community Infrastructure

Projects like this illustrate an important point: informal networks function as a form of social infrastructure within communities.

Just as physical infrastructure such as roads or water systems supports everyday life, social infrastructure supports wellbeing and resilience.

Men's Sheds, Landcare groups, volunteer fire brigades and similar organisations provide:

Purposeful activity
Participants contribute their time and skills to projects that benefit the community or environment.

Regular social contact
Shared work creates opportunities for friendships and ongoing interaction.
Intergenerational exchange
People of different ages collaborate, allowing experience and energy to complement each other.

Low-pressure conversation
Discussion occurs naturally alongside practical work rather than through formal facilitation.

These environments do not present themselves as mental health programs. Yet they can play a preventative role by strengthening community connection and reducing isolation.

Complementing Professional Support

It is important to recognise that informal support networks do not replace professional mental health care.

Counselling, psychological therapy and crisis services remain essential components of a healthy community support system. Individuals experiencing significant distress or mental health challenges should always have access to professional help.

However, informal networks can complement these services in several ways.

They can reduce stigma around discussing personal challenges. They can encourage individuals to seek professional support when needed. They can provide ongoing social connection that continues alongside formal treatment.

In this sense, community organisations and health services are not separate systems but interconnected parts of a broader wellbeing landscape.

Regeneration Takes Time

Environmental restoration offers a useful metaphor for social wellbeing.

The reed raft installed on the dam will not transform the water overnight. Roots must grow gradually. Sediment will slowly accumulate around them. Insects and birds will arrive as the habitat improves.

The process takes patience.

Similarly, the benefits of community volunteering accumulate over time. Regular participation in shared activities strengthens relationships and builds resilience.

Small actions matter.

A planted reed.

A repaired tool.

A conversation that begins while working side-by-side.

Over months and years these moments create networks of connection that support both individuals and communities.

Conclusion

Men's wellbeing is often discussed in terms of crisis response and clinical services. These remain critically important and must continue to be supported.

At the same time, the quieter structures of community life deserve greater recognition.

Men's Sheds, Landcare groups, volunteer emergency services and other community organisations create environments where people can remain purposeful, connected and engaged.

These spaces allow conversations to emerge naturally while practical work is carried out together.

Like the floating reed raft on the dam, such structures may appear simple on the surface.

Beneath that simplicity, however, they support complex networks of connection that help stabilise the social ecosystem.

Sometimes the most effective support begins with something ordinary.

A small project.

A group of people showing up.

And the willingness to work side-by-side.

The Raft and the Yabby
What a Dam Can Teach Us About Men's Wellbeing

On the surface, it was a simple project.

A small group of people gathered beside a farm dam in the Tanunda Hills to build a floating raft of reeds.

The dam had become cloudy over the years, its edges stripped of the plant life that once helped keep the water clear.

The solution was modest: a frame of pipe and shade cloth planted with aquatic reeds.

Over time the roots would grow down into the water and begin filtering the sediment.

The raft would drift gently offshore, anchored but flexible.

A small intervention.

But like many small interventions, its real significance lay beneath the surface.

The Raft

A raft is a useful metaphor for community.

From a distance, the one floating on the dam looked uncomplicated.

A rectangle of pipe supporting young reeds planted in coconut fibre. But anyone familiar with wetland restoration knows that the visible structure is only part of the system.

The real work happens underneath.

As the reeds grow, their roots stretch down into the water, forming a dense curtain that filters sediment and supports microscopic life. Insects arrive. Small aquatic creatures find shelter. The water gradually becomes clearer.

What appears simple above the surface becomes complex below it.

Community support often works the same way.

Men's Sheds, Landcare groups, volunteer fire brigades and other informal networks can look casual from the outside. People gather to repair tools, plant trees, build something or lend a hand on a small project.

Yet beneath that simplicity lies a network of connection.

People check in with each other.

Conversations happen naturally while hands are busy. Skills are shared. Experience passes quietly from one generation to the next.

Like the reed raft, these structures stabilise the environment around them.

Side-by-Side

One of the reasons these environments work so well is that they allow what might be called side-by-side wellbeing.

Many men find it easier to talk while doing something practical rather than sitting face-to-face in a formal conversation.

Fishing, repairing machinery, planting trees or building a raft creates a shared focus.

The task removes pressure.

Words arrive gradually.

A comment about retirement.

A story about a past job.

A quiet observation about how life has changed.

No one is required to explain themselves. But the space exists if they choose to.

Standing knee-deep in the dam that morning, planting reeds into coconut fibre, one of the participants said something simple: the body remembers usefulness.

It was an observation worth noting.

Physical work can calm the mind. It reconnects people to purpose in ways that abstract conversations sometimes cannot.

This does not replace professional mental health support when it is needed. Counselling and therapy remain vital resources for people facing serious challenges.

But informal environments like this can provide something equally important. A foundation of everyday connection that helps people stay grounded.

The Dam

Before the project began, the dam itself looked depleted.

The water was cloudy with suspended clay. The banks were bare. The ecosystem that once stabilised the water had gradually disappeared.

Yet the dam still held water.

Animals still visited it.

Tracks in the mud showed where kangaroos had come down to drink.

In ecological restoration, that is often enough to begin.

A system does not need to be perfect in order to recover. It only needs the right conditions.

The floating reed raft was one of those conditions.

A small structure designed to encourage larger change.

The Yabby

During the work that day, someone wondered whether there might already be yabbies in the dam.

No one had seen one.

But that did not mean they were not there.

Yabbies live quietly beneath the mud, emerging mostly at night. Their presence can go unnoticed for long periods, even in places where they are thriving.

The idea of the unseen yabby became another metaphor.

Sometimes resilience is like that.

From the outside, a person may appear uncertain or unsettled during a life transition such as retirement. Yet beneath the surface there may still be the capacity for renewal.

Supportive environments help bring that capacity into the open.

Just as the raft does not create life in the dam but simply creates the conditions where life can flourish, community networks do not manufacture wellbeing. They make space for it to grow.

Small Beginnings

At the end of the morning's work, the group stood on the dam bank with mugs of chai and gluten-free biscuits.

The raft drifted gently offshore.

The reeds were still small.

The water remained cloudy.
Then a monarch butterfly appeared, hovering briefly above the new plants.

It was only a small sign. Insects are often the first to investigate a new habitat.

But it was enough.

Restoration had begun.

In time the reeds will grow. Their roots will filter the water. Insects will gather. Birds may follow. The dam may once again resemble a functioning wetland.

The change will not happen overnight.

But the direction is clear.

What Holds

The raft and the yabby offer a simple lesson.

Healthy systems, ecological or social, rarely rely on a single solution. They depend on networks of relationships, most of which remain invisible until we look closely.

A floating raft.

A volunteer group.

A conversation that begins while working side-by-side.

Small structures can hold more than we realise.

And sometimes the most important support begins not with a formal program, but with something much simpler.

Showing up.

Doing a small job together.

And trusting that beneath the surface, something good may already be waiting.

Discussion Questions

The Raft and the Yabby

Opening Questions – The Story

1. **What moment in the story stood out to you most, and why?**

2. The dam initially appears barren but holds potential.
   What signs in the story suggest that change is already beginning?

3. Why do you think the group chose to build a floating raft rather than attempt a large immediate solution?

4. The characters spend much of the day working quietly together.
   What do you notice about the way conversations happen during shared work?

Exploring the Metaphors

5. The raft filters and stabilises the dam over time.
   What might the raft represent in terms of community or personal support?

6. The story hints that a yabby may already be living beneath the mud, unseen.
   What might the yabby symbolise about resilience or hidden strength?

7. The butterfly appears near the end of the story.
   Why do you think the author chose that moment as a sign of change?

8. The line *'the body remembers usefulness'* appears during the work at the dam.
   What do you think this means?

Side-by-Side Wellbeing

9. The story suggests that some conversations happen more easily while people are working together rather than sitting face-to-face. **Why might that be the case for some people?**

10. Have you ever had an important conversation while doing something practical (driving, fishing, building, walking)? **What made that situation easier for conversation?**

11. What kinds of activities in your community create opportunities for **side-by-side connection**?

Retirement and Life Transitions

12. Mick reflects on retirement not as stopping work but choosing meaningful work.
    What does "purpose" look like after retirement or during life transitions?

13. Why might volunteering or community involvement be important for people adjusting to retirement?

14. What are some challenges people face when the structure of work disappears?

15. Jane asks Mick how he is travelling with retirement. It is a careful, considered question: she "rarely asked anything casually". Who might be asking Jane the same question? What do partners and spouses of retiring men sometimes experience that goes unspoken or unnoticed?

Community and Informal Support

15. The story highlights the role of informal support — people showing up and working together. **Why are these informal networks important in communities?**

16. How do groups such as Men's Sheds, Landcare, volunteer fire brigades, or community gardens support wellbeing?

17. The Seeds of Hope network encourages people to ask difficult questions that may save a life. **Why can it sometimes feel difficult to start those conversations?**

Linking Informal and Formal Support

18. The story mentions both informal support and professional help such as counselling or critical incident debriefing.
    Why are both types of support important?

19. What helps create a community where people feel safe asking for help?

Looking Forward

20. The dam restoration begins with small actions — planting reeds and building a raft.
    What small actions can make a difference in strengthening community wellbeing?

21. What role can individuals play in creating supportive environments where people feel seen and valued?

22. The story ends with the idea that change has already begun beneath the water.
    Where do you see similar beginnings of positive change in your own community?

Closing Question

A reflective ending for the group discussion:

"What does the phrase 'purpose grows where people show up' mean to you?"

Discussion Guide

The Raft and the Yabby

the land remembers water
people remember purpose

Purpose of this conversation

The Raft and the Yabby explores retirement, community volunteering, environmental restoration and the quiet ways people support one another.

This discussion guide encourages reflection on how **small acts of participation and connection can strengthen both people and communities**.

Participants are welcome to share as much or as little personal experience as they feel comfortable with.

Part 1 — The Story

1. What moment in the story stayed with you the most?
2. At first the dam appears barren. What signs suggest that change is already beginning?
3. Why do you think the group chose to begin with a **small project like the floating raft** rather than a large solution?

Part 2 — The Metaphors

4. The raft filters the water slowly over time.
   What might the raft represent in terms of **community support**?
5. The story suggests a yabby may already be living beneath the mud, unseen.
   What might the yabby represent?
6. The butterfly appears near the end of the story.
   Why do you think the author included that moment?

Part 3 — Side-by-Side Wellbeing

7. The characters spend much of the day working together rather than sitting down to talk.
   Why might conversations sometimes happen more easily **side by side**?

8. Have you ever had an important conversation while doing something practical (driving, fixing something, walking, gardening)?

9. What activities in your community help people connect in this way?

Part 4 — Retirement and Purpose

10. Mick reflects that retirement is not the absence of work, but the freedom to choose meaningful work.
    What does **purpose after retirement** look like to you?

11. Why might volunteering help people adjust to life after full-time work?

12. The story follows Mick's experience of finding purpose and connection after retirement. Both partners are entering a new season of life together. What might that transition look like from Jane's side, in her daily rhythms, her sense of space, her own needs? How often do we remember to ask the partner who adjusts alongside a retiring spouse what they need?

Part 5 — Community Support

12. The story highlights informal networks such as volunteering and community projects.
    Why are these kinds of connections important for wellbeing?

13. Many communities also have organisations that support mental health awareness and suicide prevention.
    What helps create a culture where people feel comfortable checking in on each other?

14. Sometimes simply asking someone if they are going all right can make a difference.

15. Why can it feel difficult to ask that question?

Reflection

"Purpose grows where people show up."

What does this phrase mean to you?

Contemplation

The dam restoration begins with small actions such as planting reeds and building a floating raft.

In the same way, **healthy communities often grow from small acts of care and participation**.

Sometimes change begins quietly.

For example, in the text:

...and beneath the quiet water, something had already begun.

The Raft and the Yabby uses a simple narrative about restoring a farm dam to explore broader themes of purpose, volunteering and community wellbeing.

Stories often create safer entry points for conversations that might otherwise feel difficult.

Rather than asking participants to speak directly about personal experiences, the story invites reflection through shared observations about the characters, the landscape and the work being done.

The dam restoration project also provides a powerful metaphor. The floating raft of reeds represents small interventions that gradually improve an environment over time.

In a similar way, communities are strengthened through everyday acts of participation: volunteering, checking in with neighbours, and creating spaces where people can connect.

The story highlights the idea of side-by-side wellbeing.

The way conversations often unfold more naturally when people are working together on practical tasks.

This reflects the experience of many community organisations, including Men's Sheds, Landcare groups, volunteer emergency services and other local initiatives.

Importantly, the story acknowledges that informal community support exists alongside professional mental health services.

Both play important roles in creating healthy and resilient communities.

By grounding these ideas in a familiar setting, in this instance people working together beside a dam, *The Raft and the Yabby* provides a gentle but meaningful way to begin conversations about connection, purpose and community care.

Session Structure

1. Welcome and Introduction (5 minutes)

Acknowledge Country.

Example:

We acknowledge that this meeting takes place on the traditional lands of the ________________ **people**, the Traditional Custodians of this Country. We pay our respects to Elders past and present and recognise their continuing connection to land, waters and culture.

Briefly introduce the purpose of the conversation.

Example:

"This story explores how small community actions — like restoring a dam or volunteering — can support both the environment and people's sense of purpose. Today we're reflecting on the themes in the story and what they might mean for our own communities."

You may invite someone to read the opening verse aloud:

the land remembers water
people remember purpose

2. The Story
(10 minutes)

Ask a few opening questions about the narrative itself.

Suggested questions:

- What moment in the story stayed with you the most?
- What did you notice about the way the characters worked together?
- Why do you think the author focused on a small project like building the raft?

Encourage participants to speak about the story rather than personal experience initially.
This helps people warm up to the discussion.

3. Exploring the Metaphors (10–15 minutes)

Introduce the symbolic elements in the story.

Questions:

- What might the **raft** represent in terms of community or support?
- What might the **yabby beneath the mud** symbolise?
- Why do you think the author included the butterfly moment at the end?

These metaphors often help people discuss deeper ideas indirectly.

4. Side-by-Side Wellbeing (10–15 minutes)

Introduce the idea that conversations sometimes happen more easily while people are **doing something together**.

Questions:

- Why might some people find it easier to talk while working side by side?
- What activities in your community create opportunities for this kind of connection?
- Have you noticed how volunteering or shared work can build friendships?

Examples participants might mention include:

- Men's Sheds
- Landcare
- volunteer fire brigades
- community gardens
- sporting clubs
- neighbourhood projects

5. Retirement and Purpose (10 minutes)

Invite reflection on life transitions.

Questions:

- The story suggests retirement can be a shift toward choosing meaningful work. What does purpose look like after retirement?
- Why might volunteering help people during life transitions?

This conversation can often resonate strongly with mixed-age groups.

6. Community Support and Mental Health Awareness (5–10 minutes)

You might gently introduce the theme of community care.

Questions:

- What helps create communities where people look out for each other?
- Why can it sometimes feel difficult to ask someone if they are going alright?
- What role can community groups play in supporting wellbeing?

You may briefly acknowledge organisations such as:

- Seeds of Hope Suicide Prevention Network
- Men's Sheds
- volunteer services
- local health networks

This helps participants recognise that **support exists at many levels**.

Closing Reflection

End with the line from the story:

"Purpose grows where people show up."

Invite the group to reflect:

What does this phrase mean to you?

Allow a few responses before closing.

Final Thought for Participants

You may close the session with the final line of the story:

...and beneath the quiet water, something had already begun.

This reinforces the idea that **small acts of care and participation can lead to meaningful change over time.**

Facilitator Reminder

If discussions touch on personal experiences of mental health challenges, it is helpful to remind participants that **professional support is available** through local services and health providers.

Facilitators are not expected to provide counselling, but they can encourage people to seek appropriate support if needed.

Research

Overview

Research in Australia consistently shows that men's wellbeing after retirement is strengthened not through formal services alone, but through informal connections: shared work, volunteering, and mateship.

Studies of community groups such as Men's Sheds demonstrate that working side-by-side allows men to support one another in ways that feel natural and dignified.

A Few References

Academics write about it in careful language: resilience, social participation, wellbeing after retirement.

Ballinger, M.L., Talbot, L.A. and Verrinder, G.K. (2009), 'More than a place to do woodwork: A case study of a community-based Men's Shed', *Journal of Men's Health*, 6(1), pp. 20–27.

Cox, T., Hoang, H., Barnett, T. and Cross, M. (2020), 'Older Aboriginal men creating a therapeutic Men's Shed: an exploratory study', *Ageing & Society*, 40(7), pp. 1455–1468.

Fildes, D., Cass, Y., Wallner, F. and Owen, A. (2010), 'Shedding light on men: The Building Healthy Men project', *Journal of Men's Health*, 7(3), pp. 233–240.

Gee, G., Dudgeon, P., Schultz, C., Hart, A. and Kelly, K. (2014), 'Aboriginal and Torres Strait Islander social and emotional wellbeing', in Dudgeon, P., Milroy, H. and Walker, R. (eds.), *Working together: Aboriginal and Torres Strait Islander mental health and wellbeing principles and practice*. Canberra: Commonwealth of Australia.

McCausland, R., Jamieson, S.K., Robinson, V., Spencer, W., MacGillivray, P. and Andersen, M. (2023), 'Elders' perspectives and priorities for ageing well in a remote Aboriginal community', *Ageing & Society*, 45(1), pp. 31–54.

Seidler, Z.E., Rice, S.M., River, J., Oliffe, J.L. and Dhillon, H.M. (2018), 'Men's mental health services: The case for a masculinities model', *The Journal of Men's Studies*, 26(1), pp. 92–104.

Author's Reflection
A Conversation While Editing

'Do you think people will see what we were trying to say?' Sam asked.

We were sitting at the kitchen table with the laptop open between us, editing the final version of the story.

The afternoon light came in through the window and beyond the trees the dam sat quietly in the distance. The reed raft drifted gently offshore, anchored but moving with the breeze.

I leaned back in my chair.

'I think they will,' I said. 'But probably not in the way we wrote it.'

Sam laughed. 'Meaning?'

'Meaning stories land where they need to. Someone might read it because they're interested in dam restoration. Someone else might read it because they're thinking about retirement. And someone else might recognise themselves in Mick.'

Sam nodded slowly.

'That was always the point,' he said.

We sat quietly for a moment, looking at the screen.

'You know,' Sam said, 'this reminds me of your Andamooka story about men's informal support networks.'

I grinned. Delighted Sam remembered from his trip to Andamooka.

'*Andamooka Bill and the Lights on the Hill*,' I said. 'My first eBook.'

I'd written and published the eBook in 2020, pivoting from print during the pandemic, drawing on life in the South Australian outback and reflecting on men's mental health and the quiet ways communities look after each other through informal support networks.

'That story came from the same place as this one,' I told Sam. 'Watching how men support each other without necessarily calling it support.'

'Side-by-side,' Sam said.

'Exactly.'

Years earlier, I had completed Mental Health First Aid training. The course had reinforced something I had observed in many communities.

That early conversations, simple check-ins and everyday awareness can make a significant difference.

'Mental Health First Aid taught me that you don't need to be a professional to notice when someone might be struggling,' I reminded Sam. 'But you do need to be willing to ask the question.'

Sam nodded.

'The hard question.'

'Yep,' I said. 'The one people sometimes hesitate to ask.'

Sam had encountered those conversations from another perspective.

As a volunteer with the Country Fire Service, and SA Ambulance, Sam had seen how important structured support systems could be after difficult incidents.

'CFS takes that part seriously,' Sam said. 'After major call-outs there's critical incident debriefing available. People need that space sometimes.'

'Formal support matters,' I agreed.

'Absolutely.'

Sam had also spent several years volunteering with the Seeds of Hope Suicide Prevention Network in the Barossa. The organisation works within the community to raise awareness of suicide prevention and mental health, providing information, education and training.

'Seeds of Hope talks about building the capacity of the community,' Sam said. 'Helping people feel confident enough to ask difficult questions.'

'The ones that might save a life,' I said.

‘Exactly.’

Sam said, ‘The aim is not to turn everyone into counsellors, but to create a culture where people look out for one another and are not afraid to start conversations when something seems wrong.’

‘Sometimes,’ Sam said, ‘all it takes is someone asking, “Are you going alright?” and meaning it.’

I glanced toward the dam again.

‘That’s what informal support often looks like,’ I said. ‘It doesn’t always happen in a meeting room or a clinic. Sometimes it happens while people are working together.’

‘Like building a raft,’ said Sam.

‘Exactly.’

We both knew the dam project itself was small in the grand scheme of things.

A floating raft.

A handful of reeds.

A few people giving up a morning to build something useful.

But small acts can shift environments.

Land regeneration often begins that way.

So does community care.

'Men's Sheds do it,' Sam said. 'Landcare groups. Fire brigades. Volunteers everywhere.'

'Side-by-side wellbeing,' I said.

Sam grinned.

'You're going to keep using that phrase, aren't you?'

'Probably,' I replied. 'Because it describes something real.'

Many men, we had both noticed, find it easier to talk while doing something practical. Fixing a fence. Repairing machinery. Planting trees. Building a raft.

The work becomes the structure.

Conversation arrives naturally.

'And sometimes,' Sam said, 'those conversations are the ones that matter most.'

I scrolled through the final paragraphs on the screen.

'You know what I like most about the story?' I asked Sam.

'What?'

'The yabby.'

Sam laughed.

'Of course you do.'

'It's perfect,' I said. 'Something living quietly beneath the surface that nobody noticed at first.'

Sam thought about that.

'Bit like resilience.'

'Yes,' I said. 'Exactly like that.'

We both knew that stories alone cannot solve complex issues such as suicide prevention or mental health challenges.

But stories can help people recognise things they might otherwise overlook.

The raft floating on the dam.

The butterfly arriving.

The possibility that a yabby was already living beneath the mud.

Small signs that something stronger might already be there.

I looked up from the laptop.

‘Ready to publish it?’ I asked.

Sam glanced out toward the dam one more time.

‘Yeah,’ he said.

‘Reckon we are.’

Acknowledgements
The Front Cover

nicola kngwarraye butler
australian artist and writer

her work grows from the meeting places
where people gather
where stories pass from voice to voice
where landscape holds
the memory
of those who have walked before

drawing on her eastern aranda
and luritja heritage
and the lands she lives on
and travels through
nicola listens closely to country
to waterholes and dry creek beds
to red earth and shifting skies
to the quiet knowledge held in place

her art and writing
explore the living connections
between people landscape and story
the ways
community forms around shared ground
shared histories
and shared care for country

in her work
small creatures
often carry large stories

the yabby
patient beneath the mud
of a drying waterhole
speaks of endurance
of survival through harsh seasons
of life that waits quietly
beneath the surface

until the rain returns
and the country breathes again

Written for Nicola during discussions for commissioning the artwork for the cover.

Explore more of Nicola's artwork
https://nicolabutler.com

The Back Cover

sam koerner eventually
offered the image
for the back cover
though the planting day ones
linger

a motley gathering
daggy clothes
mud stitched into cuffs and knees
happy grins we could not rinse away

the all important ee vee
mostly out of frame
as if it knew
this was never about it

kate and i
hands on hips
half-laughing
half-sliding
towards the silty edge

balance uncertain
water waiting

and the raft
no bigger than a postage stamp
adrift in the wide spread
of dam water

everything small
and everything enough

Mick's story is not unusual.

Across Australia, many men rediscover purpose, connection and wellbeing through shared work, volunteering and time spent alongside others.

Sometimes the most powerful support is simply people showing up and doing something useful together.

Every story begins somewhere, but most are carried forward by people who quietly choose to take part.

This story began with a small project beside a farm dam in the Tanunda Hills. A floating raft of reeds, a handful of tools, a few people willing to spend a morning standing in the mud.

Like many worthwhile things, it was simple to describe and harder to measure.

Alongside the practical work of restoring a landscape sits another form of restoration that happens quietly in communities.

It occurs wherever people gather to lend a hand, share knowledge, or simply spend time together working toward something useful.

Across Australia, thousands of people contribute to these informal networks every day.

These groups look different, but they share the same simple principle: people showing up.

Men's Sheds create spaces where tools are repaired, projects are built and conversations unfold naturally while hands are busy.

Landcare volunteers restore waterways, plant trees and care for landscapes that sustain both people and wildlife.

Across South Australia, Country Fire Service volunteers stand ready to respond when communities face danger, supporting one another through both the intensity of emergency response and the quieter moments afterward.

State Emergency Service volunteers also embody this spirit of showing up. Responding to storms, floods and search operations, SES members provide practical help when communities need it most, strengthening both local resilience and the quiet bonds between neighbours.

Organisations such as the Seeds of Hope Suicide Prevention Network in the Barossa also play a role. Through education, training and community awareness they encourage people to ask difficult questions and to recognise when someone may need support.

Many individuals who contribute to these efforts would not describe themselves as working in mental health.

Yet their presence, attention and willingness to show up often create the conditions where wellbeing can grow.

Some support happens formally through counselling services, crisis response teams and trained professionals whose work saves lives every day.

That work is essential and deserves continued recognition and investment.

But alongside these services exists another layer of care: quieter, less visible and equally important.

It appears in small acts.

A neighbour who checks in.

A volunteer who offers a lift.

A group of people who gather to build something useful together.

These everyday contributions are the basis for the social fabric that helps communities remain resilient.

The raft on the dam is one small example of that principle.

What began as a practical solution for improving water quality became something more: a reminder that change often begins with people working side-by-side.

We acknowledge the many volunteers, community members and organisations whose quiet commitment strengthens the places where they live.

They are the people who show up.

But also, it is individuals who say to another individual, 'Hey, I'd like to support what you're doing. How can I help?'

This is where Nicola Butler fits in. Nic and I go back many years. To times before Nicola and her uncle Brian founded *Lateral Love* in Australia. I've long been an admirer of Nic's artistic talent and I am privileged to have several of her original artworks on my walls. Nic also has a fondness for yabbies, which makes her a particularly fitting supporter of this story.

Thank you to Sam and Kate for inviting me to be part of the restoration of habitat on their property.

Thank you to Jane and Mick for being participants, readers and supporters.

Thank you to Richard for insights about the importance of informal conversations within his running club.

Thank you to Tania Materne for regular physiotherapy and sharing of book ideas.

Thank you to Kelvin for supporting my publishing ambitions since 2014.

Thank you to Karen for patiently working through the digital demands of publishing.

Thank you to Joy and Kalika at Centred In Choice for meeting in Coober Pedy in September 2019, pivoting from print to digital at the beginning of the covid pandemic, and continuing to support recreation and renewal through writing and publishing.

The support of friends and family is integral to getting books out in the world.

More often than not, that is where renewal begins. In friendship, shared work, and the quiet care of land and community.

Heather Anne Gordon
Ngadjuri, Peramangk, Kaurna Country
Barossa Valley region
South Australia
https://heathergordon.com.au/

More Books
Andamooka Bill and the Lights on the Hill
ISBN 9780648823933

Published 2020 by Centred in Choice - eBook
(men's mental health – informal supports)

Tui meets Terri – a turtle tale
ISBN 9781764471138

Published 2026 by Centred in Choice – print book
(from backyard pond to living sanctuary)

www.ingramcontent.com/pod-product-compliance
Lightning Source LLC
LaVergne TN
LVHW100322210926
848480LV00003B/1217
9781764471183